WE would be pleased to correspon
with anyone wishing to buy or se
old stamps, coins, paper money, etc., o
any kind.

Do not send anything to us withou
our instructions to do so, as we will no
be responsible for same.

Always send valuable lots by regis
tered mail or express.

Prices in this list are subject to chang
without notice.

Always enclose a 2-cent stamp for re
ply, or you get no answer.

Never clean or rub up a coin, no mat
ter how black it may be.

ST. LOUIS STAMP & COIN CO.

408 Olive Street,

St. Louis, Mo.

SPECIAL NOTICE

The prices offered in this list are for fine specimens only.

A coin badly worn, plugged, pierced, scratched or damaged in any shape, cannot be called a fine specimen, which must have a sharp and bright appearance, showing each hairline to perfection. On account of the large number of specimens issued in the last two thousand years it is impossible to issue a compact list of foreign coins, but we are always pleased to inspect such pieces and make offers on the same. Do not send them on without our instructions, but first communicate with us, sending description of pieces offered. The rarity and value of a coin arises from the fact that but few pieces of certain dates were struck at the mint, or for other reasons.

The annexed prices will be paid for Coins of the United States, provided they are in good condition.

Current and uncurrent foreign coins in gold, silver and copper bought at highest market prices.

Bank of England notes, Canada silver and currency, Mexican dollars, English sovereigns, etc., bought and sold.

READ THIS

Before You Offer to Sell Your Coins.

These Coins DO NOT Bring a Premium.

The following coins command no premium, and when you find what you have are here mentioned, do not trouble the Mint officials, or us, about them.

No premium—Half dollars of any date other than those in this list; 1839 with O over date; 1853 with arrow heads at the side of date.

No premium—Quarter dollars, 1853, with arrow heads at side of date, and rays on reverse.

No premium—Twenty cents, 1875.

No premium—Dimes. Any dates other than those given, unless in very fine condition; if worn, of no value.

No premium—Half dimes; same remarks as to dimes.

No premium—Three cents, silver, 1851 to 1861.

No premium—Five cents, 1883, without cents.

No premium—Three cents, nickel, excepting 1877, Head of Liberty.

No premium—Cents, nickel, 1857 and 1858 with eagle.

No premium—Coins worn smooth, so that date does not show.

No premium—Spanish silver coins, even though 200 years old.

No premium—Nickel three-cent pieces, dated 1865 to 1873. The ones commanding a premium are of silver.

No premium—Lincoln cents with initials V. D. B.

No premium—Buffalo nickels.

Ten Dollars—Eagle.

Coinage commenced 1795; none coined in 1802, 1805 to 1837.

1795	$15.00
1796 Eight Stars Facing	17.50
1797 Small Eagle	27.50
1797 Large Eagle	15.00
1798 Six Stars Facing	30.00
1798 Four Stars Facing	30.00
1799 Large Eagle	14.00
1800 Large Eagle	14.00
1801 Large Eagle	14.00
1803 Large Eagle	14.00
1804 Large Eagle	17.50

Five Dollars—Half Eagle.

Coinage commenced 1795; none coined 1801, 1816, 1817.

1795 Small Eagle	$12.50
1795 Large Eagle	75.00
1796 Large Eagle	15.00
1797 Sixteen Stars	50.00
1797 Fifteen Stars	50.00

Five Dollars—Half Eagle (Continued).

1797 Large Eagle	$ 50.00
1798 Large Eagle	7.50
1798 Small Eagle	200.00
1799 Large Eagle	8.00
1800	7.50
1802	7.50
1803	7.50
1804	7.50
1805	7.50
1806	7.50
1807	7.50
1807 Head to left	7.50
1808	7.50
1809	7.50
1810	7.50
1811	7.50
1812	7.50
1813	7.50
1814	8.00
1815	300.00
1818	10.00
1819	150.00
1820	20.00
1821	25.00
1822	500.00
1823	25.00
1824	30.00
1825	30.00
1826	30.00
1827	30.00
1828	40.00
1829	35.00
1830	15.00
1831	15.00
1832	25.00
1833	15.00
1834 E. Pluribus Unum on reverse	20.00

Three Dollars.
Coinage 1854 to 1889.

1854 to 1862		$ 4.50
1863 to 1872		5.00
1873		20.00
1874		4.50
1875		75.00
1876		6.00
1877		6.00
1878		4.50
1879 to 1889		5.25

Two Dollars and a Half—Quarter Eagle.

Coinage commenced 1796 none coined 1799,
1800, 1801, 1809 to 1820, 1822, 1823, 1828.

1796	No Stars	$25.00
1796	With Stars	20.00
1797		35.00
1798		15.00
1802		8.50
1804		8.50
1805		7.50

Two Dollars and a Half—Quarter Eagle

(Continued.)

1806	$12.50
1807	7.50
1808	8.00
1821	15.00
1824	15.00
1825	15.00
1826	50.00
1827	12.50
1829	12.50
1830	7.50
1831	7.50
1832	7.50
1833	7.50
1834 E Pluribus Unum on reverse	40.00

U. S. Gold Dollars

Coinage 1849 to 1889.

1849 to 1854	$ 2.00
1854 to 1862	2.00
1863	5.00
1864	6.00
1865	3.50
1866 to 1872	2.50
1873 to 1874	2.00
1875	15.00
1876 to 1877	2.50
1878 to 1889	2.25
1803—1903 Louisiana Purchase Exposition. Bust of Jefferson or Mc-Kinley	2.50
1904 Lewis & Clark Exposition	2.50
1905 Lewis & Clark Exposition	2.50

U. S. SILVER COINS.

U. S. Silver Dollars.

Coinage commenced 1794; none coined 1805 to 1835, inclusive; 1837; 1874 to 1877, inclusive. Coinage discontinued 1904.

1794 ....$	40.00
1795	2.25
1796	2.25
1797	2.25
1798 Small Eagle	2.25
1798 Large Eagle....................................	2.00
1799 Large Eagle....................................	2.00
1800 Large Eagle....................................	2.00
1801 Large Eagle....................................	2.00
1802 Large Eagle....................................	2.00
1803 Large Eagle....................................	2.00
1804 Large Eagle....................................	1,000.00
1836 Liberty seated, Flying Eagle........	6.00
1838 Liberty seated, Flying Eagle........	50.00
1839 Liberty seated, Flying Eagle........	20.00
1851	27.50
1852	27.50
1854	2.50
1855	1.50
1856	1.50
1857	1.50
1858	15.00
1866 No Motto over Eagle......................	5.00
1900 Lafayette Dollar	1.75

Trade Dollars

Coinage commenced 1873; discontinued 1883.
Demonetized by the Government; they
are worth only their intrinsic value.

1873—1879 ....$ 0.65
1880—1883 .... .90

Half Dollars.

Coinage commenced 1794; none coined 1798,
1799, 1800, 1804, 1816.

1794 ....$ 2.50

1795 ....$ 0.90
1796 .... 20.00
1797 .... 17.50
1801 .... 2.00
1802 .... 2.00
1815 .... 2.00
1836 Edge milled.. 1.50
     Note—The 1836 half dollar with
     Letters on edge commands no pre-
     mium.
1838 Liberty cap, having O between bust
     and date 150.00
1852 Liberty seated 1.00
1853 Without small arrows on each side
     of date 75.00

Quarter Dollars

Coinage commenced 1796; none coined 1797 to
1803, inclusive; 1808 to 1814, inclusive;
1816, 1817, 1826, 1829, 1830.

1796		$ 2.00
1804		1.00
1823	Head to left	15.00
1827	Head to left	20.00
1853	No arrows at each side of date and no sun rays back of eagle	4.00

20-Cent Pieces.

Coinage commenced 1875; discontinued 1878.

1876		$ 0.25
1877		2.00
1878		2.00

Dimes.

Coinage commenced 1796; none coined 1799; 1806, 1808, 1810, 1813, 1815 to 1819, inclusive; 1826.

1796	$ 1.00
1797	1.50
1798	1.50
1800	1.50
1801	2.00
1802	2.00
1803	1.50
1804	4.00
1805	.25

1807	$ 0.25
1809	.50
1811	.30
1822	1.00
1846	.20

Half Dimes.

Coinage commenced 1794; discontinued 1873; none coined 1798, 1799, 1804, 1806 to 1828.

1794	$ 1.50
1795	.50

Half Dimes (Continued).

1796	$ 1.50
1797	1.25
1800	.60

1801	$ 1.35
1802	100.00
1803	1.25
1805	2.00
1846	.50
1864	.15

Silver 3-Cent Pieces.

Coined 1851 to 1873.

1863	$ 0.40
1864	.60
1865	.40
1866	.40
1867	.40
1868	.40
1869	.40

1870	$ 0.40
1871	.40
1872	.40
1873	.50

Nickel 5-Cent Pieces.

Coinage commenced 1866.

1877 ....$ 1.00
1878 .... .10

Nickel 3-Cent Pieces.

Coined 1865 to 1889.

1877 ....$ 1.50

Copper 2-Cent Pieces.

Coined 1864 to 1873.

1873 ....$ 1.50

Copper Cents.

Coinage commenced 1793; discontinued 1857;
none coined 1815.

1793 Liberty, chain ....$ 2.00
1793 Liberty, wreath... 2.00
1793 Liberty, cap 2.00
1794 .... .10
1795 .... .10

Copper Cents (Continued).

1796 Liberty, cap.................................$ 0.25
1796 Fillet head 25
1797 05
1798 05

1799 ....$ 4.00
1804 ....   3.00
1805 10
1806 25
1808 10
1809 50
1811 25
1813 20
1821 10
1823 10
1857 07

1856 Flying Eagle, copper-nickel..................$5.00

Half Cents.

Coinage commenced 1793; discontinued 1857;
none coined 1798, 1799, 1801, 1812 to 1824;
1827, 1830, 1837, 1838, 1839.

1793		$ 1.00
1794		.20
1795		.30
1796		5.00
1797		.50
1802		.75
1810		.10
1811		.35
1831		10.00
1836		10.00
1840		10.00
1841		10.00
1842		10.00
1843		10.00
1844		10.00
1845		10.00
1846		10.00
1847		10.00
1848	Head to left	10.00
1849	Head to left, small dates	10.00
1852	Head to left	10.00

For all other dates of half cents
we pay 10 cents each.

COLONIAL COINS.

Silver Colonial Coins.

1652 New England shilling..............................$10.00
1652 New England sixpence.......................... 15.00
1652 New England threepence..................... 25.00

1652 Pine Tree, Mass., shilling....................$ 2.00
1652 Pine Tree, Mass., sixpence................... 2.00
1652 Pine Tree, Mass., threepence............... 2.00
1662 Pine Tree, Mass., twopence................... 2.00
1652 Mass. Oak Tree, shilling....................... 1.00
1652 Mass. Oak Tree, sixpence..................... 1.50
1652 Mass. Oak Tree, threepence................. 2.00
1652 Mass. Oak Tree, twopence.................... 2.00
1659 Lord Baltimore shilling....................... 10.00

1659 Lord Baltimore sixpence..................$ 7.50

Silver Colonial Coins (Continued).

1659 Lord Baltimore fourpence.................$12.50
1783 U. S. 1000 Eye Nova Constellatio...... 75.00
1785 U. S. 500 Eye Nova Constellatio,
    quarter dollar 75.00
1785 Justice Eye Nova Constellatio,
    quarter dollar 40.00
1790 Head Standish Barry, threepence...... 5.00
1783 Annapolis shilling 2.00
1783 Annapolis sixpence 5.00
1783 Annapolis threepence 5.00

Tin Colonial Coins.

1776 $1.00 Sundial Continental currency....$2.00

Copper Colonial Coins.

1721 Louisiana Cent ....$ 0.15
1767 Louisiana Cent .... .15
    U. S. A. Bar Cent.................................... 1.00
1722 Rosa American twopence..................... .50
1722 Rosa American penny.......................... .25
1722 Rosa American half penny.................. .40
1783 U. S. (eye) Nova Constellatio cent .20
1785 U. S. (eye) Nova Constellatio cent .15
1787 Sundial-links, "We are one," Frank-
    lin cent .... .10

New York Cents.

1786 Eagle, Excelsior...$ 7.50
1786 Head, Justice, Non Vi Virtue Vici.... 30.00
1787 Indian, Eagle, Nova Eboracus............. 10.00
1787 Arms of N. Y., Excelsior....................... 7.50
1787 Head Liberty, Nova Eboracus............. .15
1787 Justice, Eagle, Immunis Columbia.... 1.50

New Hampshire Cents.

1776 Cent, tree and harp..............................$20.00

New Jersey Cents.

1786 Horse Head, Shield, Nova Caes-
 area ....$ 0.10
1787 Justice, Shield, Immune Columbia.... 10.00

Vermont Cents.

1785 Head, Justice, Immune Columbia.......$ 1.50
1785 Eye, Justice, Immune Columbia......... 10.00
1785 Eye, Sun, Vermontis, Republica......... .20
1786 Eye, Sun, Vermontensium Repub-
 lica .... .25

Massachusetts Cents.

1787 Indian, Eagle, cent...............................$ 0.10
1788 Indian, Eagle, cent............................... .15
1787 Indian, Eagle, half-cent....................... .25
1788 Indian, Eagle, half-cent....................... .25

Connecticut Pieces.

1785 to 1788, inclusive, Auctori Connect....$ 0.08
1737—39 Deer, "Value me as you please,
 I cut my way through," Granby
 threepence 10.00

Washington Pieces.

SILVER.

1792 Half dollar, 15 stars..............................$25.00
1792 Half dollar, large eagle, no stars...... 25.00

COPPER CENTS

1783 Liberty seated, U. S..............................$ 0.20
1783 Head larger, U. S.............................. .20
1783 Head Unity, U. S.............................. .15
1785 Head Confederatio 25.00
1791 Large eagle 1.50

1791 Small eagle ....$ 1.50
1792 Naked bust right.............................. 10.00
1793—95 Head, ship, half-penny.............................. .30
1793 Head, harp, half-penny, N. Wales.... .35
1791 Head, ship, half-penny, Liverpool.... .40

CALIFORNIA GOLD

1853—75 California gold dollars, either
round or octagonal.................................$ 2.25
1852—81 California gold half dollars,
either round or octagonal.................. .90
1852—81 California gold quarter dollars,
either round or octagonal.................. .75

Fifty-Dollar Slugs—Octagon.

1851 Augustus Humbert, octagonal..........$ 90.00
1851 U. S. Assay office.................................. 90.00
1851 50 in center of reverse......................... 100.00
1852 Augustus Humbert 90.00

Fifty-Dollar Slugs—Round.

1854 Wass Molitor & Co..............................$150.00
1855 Kellogg & Co... 300.00

Twenty-Dollar Pieces.

1851 Baldwin & Co.....................................$100.00
1853 Moffat & Co.. 22.00
1853 U. S. Assay Office.............................. 21.00
1854-55 Kellogg & Co................................. 21.00
1855 W. M. & Co... 35.00

California Gold (Continued).
Ten-Dollar Pieces.

1849 Moffat & Co...$ 11.50
1849 Cincinnati Mining & Trading Co..... 125.00
1849 Pacific Co.. 150.00

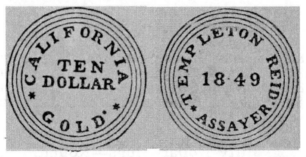

1849 Templeton Reid $200.00

1850 Baldwin & Co..$75.00

California Ten-Dollar Gold (Continued).

1851 Baldwin & Co.................................$100.00
1850 Dubosq & Co.................................. 200.00
1852 August Humbert 12.00
1852 Moffat & Co.................................. 11.00

    No date, Miners Bank.....................$ 35.00
1852 U. S. Assay Office........................ 11.00
1852 W. M. & Co................................. 13.50
1853 U. S. Assay Office.......................... 11.00
    No date, J. S. O............................ 100.00
1855 W. M. & Co................................. 15.00

Five-Dollar Pieces.

1849 Moffat & Co..............................$ 6.00

1849 Pacific Co. $150.00

California Five-Dollar Gold (Continued).

1849 Cincinnati Mining & Trading Co......$150.00
1849 Mass. & California Co........................ 150.00

1849 N. G. & N..$ 11.00
1850 Baldwin & Co....................................... 15.00
1850 Dubosq & Co.. 75.00
1850 Moffat & Co... 6.00
1851 Dunbar & Co.. 75.00

1851 Shults & Co... 75.00
1852 W. M. & Co..$ 12.50
25.00 Templeton Reid 500.00

COLORADO GOLD.

Twenty-Dollar Pieces.

1860 Clark Gruber & Co...........................$100.00
1861 Clark Gruber & Co........................... 50.00

Ten-Dollar Pieces.

1860 Clark Gruber & Co...........................$ 20.00
1861 Clark Gruber & Co........................... 12.50
  No date, J. J. Conway & Co............ 250.00

Five-Dollar Pieces.

1860 Clark & Co...................................$ 7.50
1861 Clark Gruber & Co...........................   7.50
  No date, John Parsons & Co........... 200.00
  No date, J. J. Conway & Co........... 100.00

Two-and-a-Half Dollar Pieces.

1860 Clark & Co...................................$ 6.50
1861 Clark Gruber & Co...........................   7.00
  No date, John Parsons & Co........... 125.00
  No date, J. J. Conway & Co........... 200.00

UTAH MORMON GOLD.

1849 $20.00 Clasped Hands.........................:$125.00
1849 10.00 Clasped Hands.................:....... 150.00
1849   5.00 Clasped Hands........................ 12.00
1850   5.00 Clasped Hands........................ 12.00

1860 $5.00 Lion ....$ 25.00

1849 $2.50 Clasped Hands...................:...........$ 15.00

OREGON GOLD.

1849 $10.00 Oregon Exchange Co..............$200.00
1849   5.00 Oregon Exchange Co.............: 35.00

CAROLINA GOLD

No date, $5.00 A. Bechtler...........................$10.00
No date, 5.00 C. Bechtler........................... 12.00
No date, 5.00 North Carolina gold, C.
    Bechtler 17.50
1834 $5.00 A. Bechtler............................ 12.00
1834 5.00 C. Bechtler............................ 12.00
No date, $2.50 Carolina gold, Bechtler...... 10.00
No date, $2.50 North Carolina gold, C.
    Bechtler 10.00
No date, $2.50 North Carolina gold,
    Bechtler 10.00
No date, $1.00 Carolina, Bechtler............... 1.50
No date, $1.00 A. Bechtler.......................... 2.00

GEORGIA GOLD.

$10.00 Templeton Reid $150.00
  5.00 Templeton Reid 100.00
  5.00 C. Bechtler Georgia gold.............. 15.00
  2.50 Templeton Reid 40.00
  2.50 Bechtler 10.00

www.ingramcontent.com/pod-product-compliance
Lightning Source LLC
LaVergne TN
LVHW011026040625
813000LV00009B/532